Mia Masuzaka 1st Photo Book
LOCATION IN MIYAKOJIMA

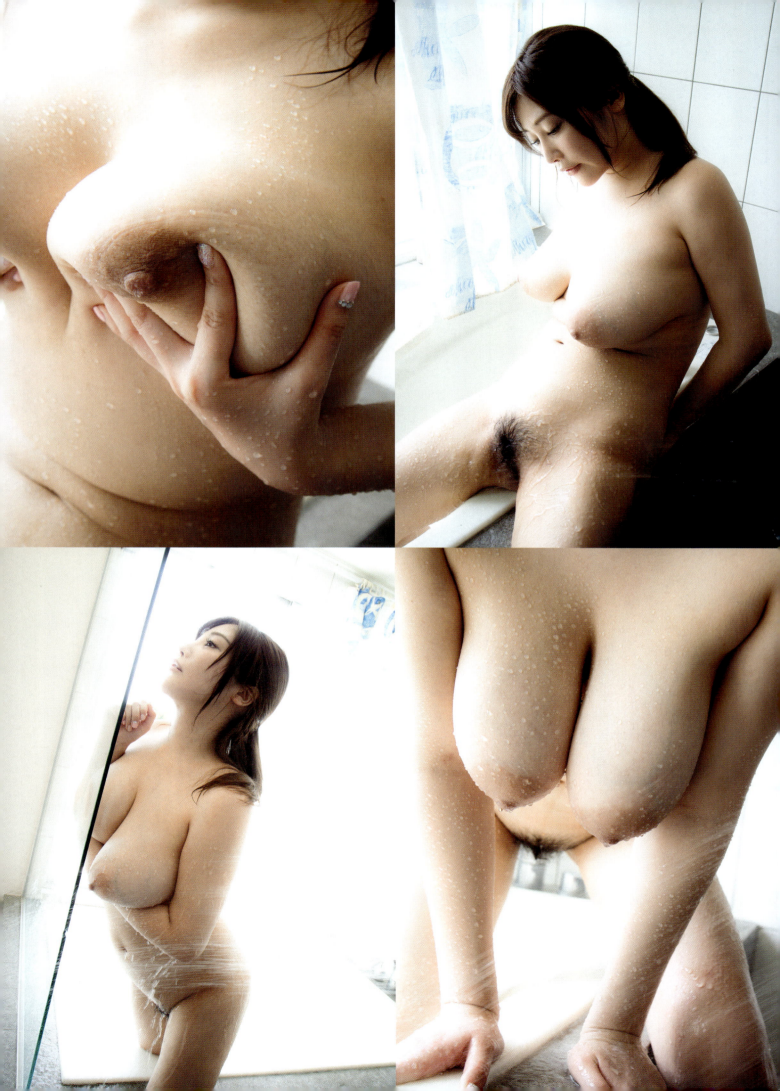

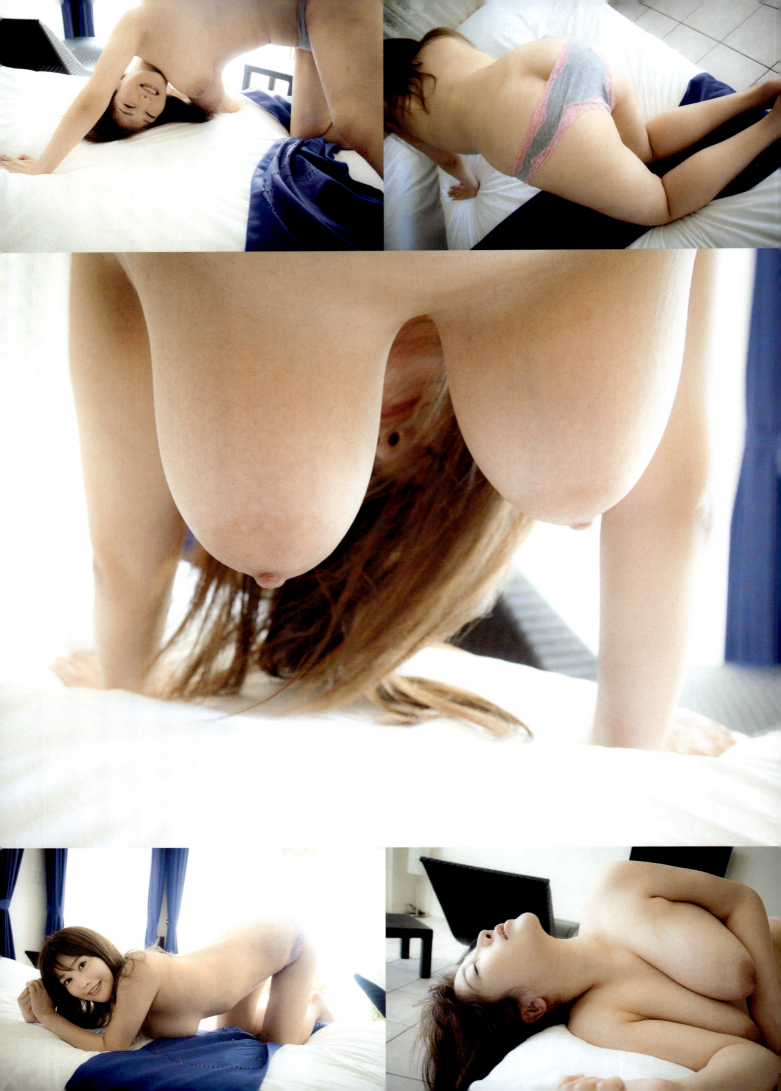

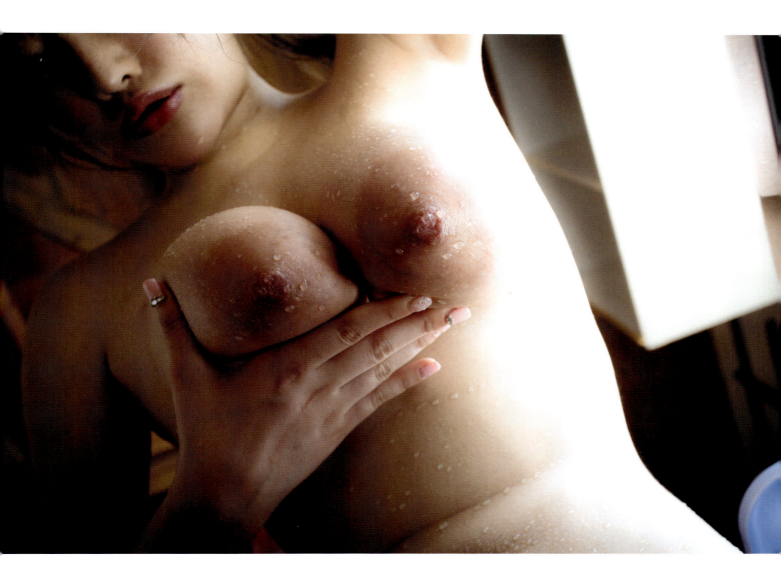

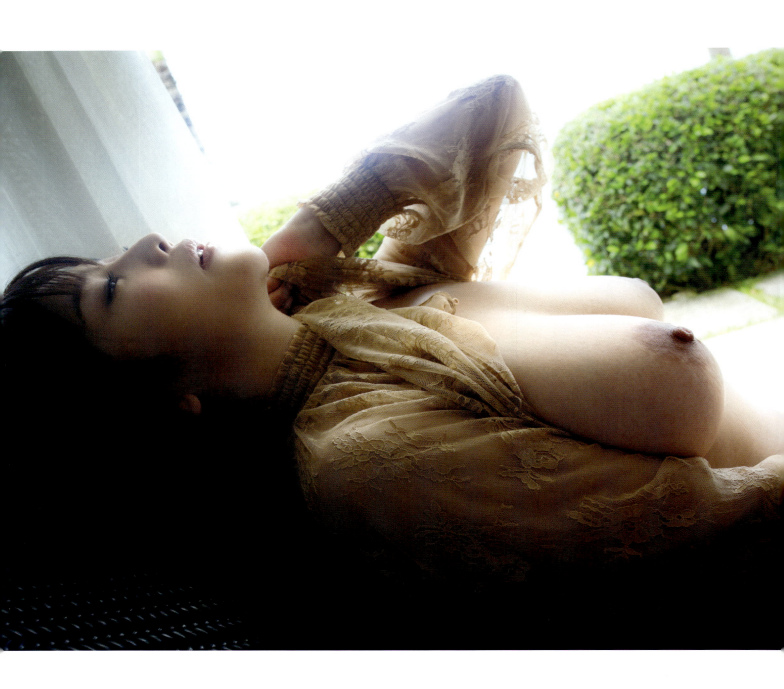

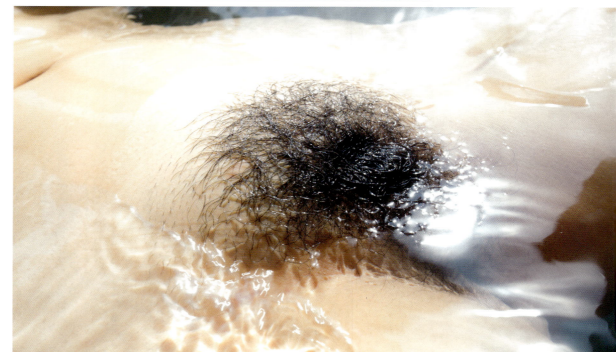

MIA MASUZAKA
FIRST
PHOTO BOOK

LOCATION IN MIYAKOJIMA

Artist: MIA MASUZAKA
Photographer: SUSUMU MAKIHARA
Assistant Photographer: RINTARO URYU
Styling: MIA MASUZAKA & ISAKO TOSHIKUNI
Hair and make-up: ISAKO TOSHIKUNI
Artist Management: SABURO MATSUI (C-more)
　　　　　　　　　 KATSUHITO ABE (C-more)
Art Director: RYOTA MIZUKI
Editor: HIROSHI SHIBATA (TAKESHOBO)

本書の無断複写・複製・転載を禁じます。
定価はカバーに表記してあります。

©2018 Takeshobo Co.,Ltd.

※【特典チェキ】はカメラの性質上、写りが多少ボケていたりするのもありますがご了承ください。
また特典チェキに関する苦情・クレーム等に関しては受け付けておりませんので宜しくお願いします。